25

Starters

Dre Baldwin

Dre Baldwin

Copyright © 2016 Work On Your Game Inc.

ISBN: 1539071907
ISBN-13: 978-1539071907

DEDICATION

To you, for being ready to break out of your shell and start communicating.

CONTENTS

Dre Baldwin

INTRODUCTION

Conversation is simple and easy.

We share things with others, and others share things with us. It doesn't always work out this simply, of course, but this is who we are at our cores. Humans are social creatures; we share.

Verbal communication played a significant role in all your biggest life achievements. The sexiest guy or girl you've dated. The most money you ever made. The happiest you've ever been. Didn't all of these come, in whole or in part, from some amount of conversation?

Who are your best friends? Your closest relatives? And how did they become so close and important to you? From conversation!

So, knowing how important conversation is, why do so many of us struggle with it?

We think too damn much.

About?

What the other person might think of us.

How we might sound stupid.

If this is a dumb question.

Possibly being turned down for something.

The fear of the unknown.

Eliminate these fears, and conversation is easy. These fears are mostly based in a lack of knowledge. A lack of knowledge in how to start a conversation and how to keep conversation flowing. But, you picked up this book.

And that fear will be gone very soon.

***

Verbal communication is the skill which keeps humans at the top of the food chain. We aren't winning based on size, speed or strength! Without our advanced communication skills, we would be prey to the many bigger, stronger and faster animals we see on National Geographic.

The most successful people we know (of) are the best communicators.

They're the people who can best get their point across. The ones who are good at persuasion. The people who can make people feel things - happiness, anger, sadness, motivation. The best communicators make their every communication feel like a personal conversation with you.

Is this true or not true?

Since you agree, would you also agree that an improvement in your conversational skills would boost your success in life?

Good. You have the perfect tool for doing so.

This book shares 25 great conversation starters guaranteed to get people talking.

These questions will make your conversation companion think and talk more. These are not the usual stereotypical, boring questions bad conversationalists use all the time, such as *Where are you from?* Or, *What do you do?* The starters in this book are pattern-interrupting ways to get a person deep in thought and talking.

Why is this important?

1. Questions that make people think get their attention. Attention and time are the most valuable currencies we deal in.

2. The more you can talk with someone, the better you can learn how to help him or her. Helping people creates value, and we will pay high prices for value.

3. Unique, thought-provoking conversation makes people remember you. I doubt you want to be a forgotten person.

These conversation starters facilitate *further* conversation, which you can leverage to get your point across, build rapport, learn about others, win friends and influence people.

So, to this point, what about this book has you most excited? Why is that?

***

Each chapter is headed with the conversation starter itself, and then a simple background on the value of the question, *written in italics*.

Then, I'll give more context into what results to expect from the question and what to listen for.

I'll share a few **Follow Up** questions to use, based on the answers you get. It's important you learn to weave the follow-ups into conversation, and not sound like an interviewer or news reporter following a memorized script.

At the end of each chapter, you'll get a **Best Used** tip for best times to employ each question and why.

Warning: Do not use these conversation starters as a memorized, systematic way of talking to people. Learn them all and learn to use them together and independently as needed. The more you go over each, you will develop a feel for when and how to use each.

Let's get started and not waste time. There are people to meet and connections to make.

1 WHAT BRINGS YOU TO _____?

An easy ice breaker.

This open question allows you to find out a person's motivation for being where you are.

Maybe she knows the host of the event. Maybe she is new in town and looking to make new friends. Perhaps her girlfriend heard about the event (or club or team or Meetup) and dragged her out too.

Everyone is where they are for a reason, thus everyone has an answer for this question.

Follow Ups:

What do you hope to get from being here?

How did you find out about this?

If you came here agin, who would you bring with you?

Best Used: At gatherings or events where people choose to show up, and it's not a normal thing. Think parties, networking events, art festivals.

You would not use this at a place you could reasonably expect people to be at regularly, such as a grocery store or community swimming pool. Think of how silly it sounds. *So, what brings you to Whole Foods today?*

2 WHERE DO YOU SEE YOURSELF GOING IN THE NEXT 3-5 YEARS?

This is a pattern-breaking question which most people have never been asked. It will get them thinking and will also make them remember you, as the one who asked it.

This is a great way to begin to discern what kind of person you're talking to.

Does he have goals for his life?

Has he considered his future, or is he just drifting along day by day?

Are his aspirations completely different from his current reality? This could denote ambition or delusion, but you will learn more over time.

Follow Ups:

What do you feel you most need, to make sure you get there in that time frame?

How much do you think you'll need to change as a person to achieve this?

How confident are you today about getting there?

Best Used: In conversation after some level of rapport has been established. This is not one of the first questions you ask a person, even if you're running a job interview. You're asking someone to tell you their hopes, goals and dreams - we don't usually share these with complete strangers! Make sure you're not a stranger anymore *before* you ask this.

3 OF PEOPLE YOU KNOW, WHO DO YOU ADMIRE THE MOST AND WHY?

The value in people is not only in the person herself - it's in who she knows. This question will open the door to those people. You'll also lean what and who she values by her answer.

People are a resource whose value increases the more of them you have in your circle. There is no downside to knowing more people tomorrow than you know today. The answer someone gives to this question shares how your subject thinks, and who she may know who you may want to know.

Take note of not only *who* the answer is, but *why*. The *why* part tells you what she considers admirable. Do you also have the same trait? Do you know someone who does?

Does she admire someone because of his money?

Because a person donates to charity?

Because her mom raised her as a single parent?

Because some guy died in while on a military tour of duty?

Follow Ups:

How long have you admired this person?

Do you ever ask this person for advice or guidance?

If you could adopt one trait from this person, what would it be and why?

Best Used: When rapport is strongly established and you want to keep the conversation going. This question can get a person talking - a lot. Make sure you're ready and available for that before you pull this one out.

4 OF PEOPLE YOU DO NOT KNOW, WHO DO YOU ADMIRE THE MOST AND WHY?

This is a simple flip on #3, and a question that tells you something important: What do you value in someone whom you don't even know?

The traits or actions a person admires in someone whom they don't even know could show how much they value surface traits (such as hair color, big muscles, nice car or clothes) or heresy stories (some story perpetrated by the media that has never been confirmed). It could also be that they admire an idea the admired person espouses (world peace, taking care of family, doing big business).

The answers you hear tells you the ideas and ideals of the person who shares. Think of a person you admire whom *you* don't know. Why do you admire this person? Is your admiration based on facts, something you feel, or something you heard? Maybe it's an idea this person represents, or one profound thing he or she said once?

Follow Ups:

How much of this person do you see in yourself?

How long have you admired this person?

If you could meet this person, what would you most want to talk about?

Best Used: Same situation as #3. Rapport is established and you are prepared and available for a conversation to extend and continue.

5 WHAT IS THE BIGGEST CHALLENGE YOU FACE IN BUSINESS THESE DAYS?

Everyone works or is trying to find work. Find out what kind of work they're doing and where help is needed.

This questions kills the bland, overused *what do you do?* question that lazy conversationalists repeatedly throw around.

Not only will you find out what he does, but also what problems he's facing in doing it.

No one's work or business is ever perfect, which is why this is a great question - there's *always* an answer. And you're creating an opening for someone to share how he could possibly be helped. This is an opportunity for you to provide value, with your own skill, or the connection to someone else who can help. There is tremendous value in being a broker between people.

Follow Ups:

How long has this been a challenge?

What do you think is the quickest/easiest way to solve it?

When this is resolved, how will that help you/your business? What does it allow you to do then?

What challenges remain after this one is handled?

Best Used: When talking business or work with someone. This is especially useful when you feel someone is trying to corner you with a ton of questions about *your* business. This questions flips the situation around quickly.

This is a pattern interrupt that will break any line of questioning directed towards you. He has to think to answer, and will lose his train of thoughts in questioning you. Use this starter offensively, to take the focus off of you and put it on whomever you ask it to. Everyone will be looking at the person who was asked, awaiting his answer.

6 WHAT ARE THE 3 BEST THINGS ABOUT YOUR LINE OF WORK?

Another one to get them thinking, and inadvertently selling their work or business to you.

This will get a person to tell you why she does what she does - or at least why she did at first!

You'll also learn what really matters to a person. We spend 1/3 of our lives working. The things that makes that work worthwhile to a person tells you a lot about who she is as a person. *Here's why I spend 1/3 of my life doing this!*

This answer will tell you why, even if her current work isn't what she wants to do ultimately.

Let's say for example, she works the register at McDonald's but wants to be a lawyer. Her 3 Best Things may be to pay for college, take care of her 2 year old son, and because work close to home.

So you learned that she's in school (Where? For how long?), has a child (What's his name? Do you have photos? Married to his father?) and lives close to a McD's (what neighborhood? Do you not have a car?). These answers and follow up questions keep a conversation flowing. Amongst all these questions and her answers, you'll learn a lot and have plenty of material with which to keep talking.

Follow Ups:

Would you advise someone to join your line of work today? Why or why not?

Do you think most people even know about these 3 best things? Why or why not?

If these 3 things went away, would you still do what you do? (may or may not be applicable, depending on line of work)

Best Used: 1) When you want to learn how you can help someone. 2) To cheer someone up who is complaining about her job - get her thinking about what's good about it! 3) Taking attention off yourself; especially useful in a group setting.

7 DID YOU ALWAYS KNOW YOU WOULD BE IN THE _____ FIELD/INDUSTRY?

Are you living your dreams, or did they take a detour to where you are now? Or do you still not know what you ultimately want?

I've used this question literally hundreds of times. Sadly, the common reply from people is, they're not doing what they always thought they would be doing.

This is good news for you though: You now have more conversation material!

The answers to this question will take you into someone's history, their regrets and failures.

Very rarely is someone satisfied with not being or doing what he always thought he'd be or be doing. You'll have him thinking about things he probably doesn't think of too often.

As he opens up to you, answering in itself will make him feel more of a connection to you. Since he's opening up about his life to you, you must be a likable fellow. Why else would he be telling you his business? We call this confirmation bias: We alter our feelings to confirm our actions, and vice-versa.

We don't share this kind of stuff with people we don't have a connection with, so you *must* be trustworthy.

Follow Ups:

When did your current work become a possibility for you?

What caused you to not be doing what you always thought you'd be doing?

Are you still pursuing it?

How long will you _____ (be a waitress, sell insurance, do maintenance)?

What's the biggest challenge to you getting where you want to be? Anything I can do to help?

What's next for you?

Best Used: When you're really getting to know someone. This is good for a second conversation, or a first conversation that goes long and deep.

Be careful not to pull this out too soon, as a person can become defensive or evasive and not give you a real answer. If this happens, it will be hard for him to go back and give you a different answer, which would make him appear to be dishonest. By using this question at the right time, you protect him from having to lie to you.

8 WHAT CAN I DO TO HELP YOUR BUSINESS?

An offer of help puts you in a position of power, at least temporarily. If you've demonstrated enough value in yourself to this point, you may be taken up on this offer.

Understand: Offering to help someone's business does not necessarily mean free help.

We pay mechanics to help us with our cars. We pay childcare centers to help us in looking after our children. We pay trainers to help us with our physical fitness.

Whether she inherently understands this or not depends on how you present yourself in conversation or your prior reputation.

If she doesn't inherently understand, no worries - tell her explicitly!

I can help you by redoing your website? Great! I offer 3 website design packages…

I can help you by creating a custom meal plan? Great! I sell 3 month, 6 month and 12 month meal plans…

YES, I can help you by watching your 2 and 4 year old kids this Friday! I baby sit for $35/hour. What's your home address and what time should I arrive?

No one's business is 100% perfect; we all have areas of work we could improve. When you ask how you can help, you may be countered with, *what do you specialize in?* Or, *what do you do exactly?* Or, *what do you do best?*

Be as specific as possible in your reply (or explanation of your work beforehand) to make it easy for her to envision using your help.

Follow Ups:

How long has this been a need?

Do you have people/places/things in mind that could make this a reality?

What will this do for your business, and why does that matter?

Best Used: When near to closing a conversation. This opens the door for a follow up action or conversation. At the very least, you've left the door open for this person to contact you again.

9 DESCRIBE THE IDEAL PERSON YOU'RE LOOKING TO WORK WITH RIGHT NOW.

Let him tell you exactly what or who he needs right now.

Asking a person to talk out who or what he needs helps him more than it even helps you.

Most people have never fully laid out who or what they need. Describing this ideal person lets him consider exactly what he would need from them, or if it's even feasible to get so much from one person - maybe he needs 3 or 4 people!

Talking about it with you may also lead to a "lightbulb" moment for him, such as *I don't even need anyone else* or *I already know the perfect person!*

Follow Ups:

How do you know this is the ideal person to work with?

What does this person bring to the table that you don't?

Where would you find such a person?

How much time commitment would you need?

What kind of salary or hourly pay would you offer the right person? (This gives insight for you to possibly connect someone to him)

Best Used: When you're closing a conversation and looking for a way to provide value and consider future follow up. With this information in hand, you can be on the lookout for that ideal person and play the broker between both people. You could also offer some ideas for where he could find this person, if it won't be through you.

10 WHAT DID YOU WANT TO BE WHEN YOU WERE GROWING UP?

How ambitious and self-starting is this person? How much does "reality" (the bad, dream-shattering kind) control him?

This is a play on #7, coming from the other end of the question. This is asking, *what was your ideal back then?* As opposed to, *how does the current reality compare with the old ideal?*

So instead of current-reality mode, put him in dream mode. Compare his answer with the person you see in front of you. Take note of the seriousness of his non-verbal cues as he replies. This could help you infer if he ever really went for it, or if was always a far away fantasy.

Follow Ups:

How long did you have that dream/goal/idea?

Did you tell anyone about it, and how did they respond?

(If you know for sure he did not become it) When did you change your mind?

(If you're not sure if he became it, or think he still could) Do you still see that as your future? What's the next step to you getting there?

Best Used: This one is versatile. You can use it as an icebreaker to start a conversation, in the middle to revive conversation, or an attention deflector in a group or when you feel you're being grilled by a person or multiple people.

11 ARE YOU HERE ALONE LIKE I AM?

Break the ice when you're alone and they are, too.

It's funny - when someone is somewhere alone, and another person is also alone, they're both apprehensive about approaching.

But when they're both with companions, it seems easier to talk to strangers.

This conversation starter makes it easier in those alone times.

Say this confidently and with a friendly smile. You'll get a smile back, and an expectation to keep the conversation going. You could introduce yourself here, or ask something else simple like, *is this seat taken? Or, what brings you here?*

The introduction can come after those softball openers. Use them both ways, and learn to weave them as needed.

This question creates instant rapport since you two have something in common. It also establishes you as a leader (of two people) since you confidently initiated the conversation. Be ready to carry it now with more good questions.

Even if she's *not* alone, your confident approach and question establishes that you *are* alone, and maybe you'll be invited into a conversation.

If not, move on to another person!

Follow Ups:

What brings you here?

Who's the ideal person you'll meet here?

Who do you know who should *be here, but is not?*

Best Used: When you're alone at an event where some people do know each other. Think Meet-ups, art or music festivals, parties and get-togethers.

This is *not* best used at places where everyone is essentially alone, like a school orientation, as it would be too obvious.

12 WHAT ARE YOU LOOKING TO GET OUT OF THIS _____ (EVENT, SCHOOL YEAR, DAY, CONFERENCE)?

Find out a person's motivations. Motives control behavior.

This is a direct-but-open question for you to learn *why* someone is doing what he's doing. People don't do things for no reason. His answer lets you in on the reasons, which contain information all their own. Keep listening.

If the answer is empty - *I was forced to be here, I have no idea what this is all about, I really don't know* - you have more ammunition to keep talking with. Find out why!

Follow Ups:

How did you find out about this?

Have you been here before?

How/Why do you think you can get that here?

How will _____ (getting some outcome from this event) help you?

Why is that outcome important?

Best Used: When talking to someone you've just met at any type of event which people attend voluntarily. Wine tastings, speed dating, college orientation, business expos.

13 WHAT'S YOUR BEST SKILL?

When does this person see herself at her best? What can you learn from it?

Asking someone what her best skill is leads to several new pieces of info.

1. What she's most proud of

2. Asking yourself if you can visualize her using this skill in her daily life

3. If you have something in common with her skill

4. If you know someone who could benefit from her skill

5.   How confident and clear is she in answering

Asking someone a question which allows her to shine and talk herself up is always a good strategy. Use this often as this question will make you new friends quickly. People rarely get to talk proudly of themselves to someone who is actually listening.

Follow Ups:

How do you know it's your best skill?

When did you realize this?

What's the ultimate outcome you want to get from your ability?

Best Used: When trying to open up someone who is less forthcoming in conversation. Talking about what we're good at causes anyone to light up - as long as we have a willing listener.

14 WHAT'S YOUR BIGGEST WEAKNESS?

People will answer this in one of two ways. Which one, depends completely on how comfortable she is with you at this point.

Everyone has good weaknesses and real weaknesses.

Good weaknesses are the weaknesses we share in job interviews. *I work too hard. I am a perfectionist. I'm very demanding of anyone who works with me. I try too hard to make people happy.*

Real weaknesses are... *real* weaknesses. *I am not a strong leader. I get too emotional at times. I get nervous in front of groups. I have anger issues. I really wish I had more confidence.* This is the stuff we get very good at masking and unconsciously minimizing. These, we aren't always so forthcoming with.

Some people are more open books than others; these are the types to answer the weakness question honestly within 20 minutes of meeting you. These people are more empathetic and will connect with you also when you communicate your feelings and emotions. With these types, use phrases such as *I feel/felt, that bothers me, I'm so happy!*

Others can be more guarded and will never give you the real answer (but a keen observer can notice this, over time). These people will communicate (at first, at least) more by hard observation - facts, figures, knowledge, black-and-white.

Follow Ups:

Why is it a weakness?

When has this weakness cost you?

What do you do to compensate for the weakness?

Best Used: After you've established rapport and feel a person has opened up to you.

Know what type of person you're dealing with and what stage you're at with her (open or closed with her feelings). Timing is important: used too early, you may get a good weakness and never a real one. If you get a good weakness early, sharing a real one later may make someone feel like a liar. So don't make this mistake of asking too soon.

You may need some time with a person to really use this question.

15 WHAT WAS YOUR BIGGEST FAILURE?

What's her lowest low? How does she feel about it?

When you get an answer to this (almost everyone will answer it), notice the non verbal cues she gives off. Does she go back to the feeling of that time? Can she freely talk about it as if it happened to someone else? Is she completely open in talking about it? Or does she hesitate to even bring it up?

These cues will tell you 1) how in touch with her feelings she is, and 2) how comfortable she feels talking to you right now (which will affect #1).

Depending on how the question is answered, you have options in your follow up.

Follow Ups:

How did it happen?

What did you do next?

How did you go from there to here?

How long did it take to get over that?

Why is that your biggest failure?

Best Used: Again, when you have built solid rapport with your conversation partner. Ask too early, and risk getting a surface, "safe" response that is too easy to explain (and not the real answer).

16 WHAT IS THE BEST ADVICE YOU'VE EVER GOTTEN?

Learn a principle of life that guides her actions to this very day.

The best advice someone ever got is likely something she still abides by now. It doesn't matter how long ago it was, as she is still recalling it to this day.

Follow Ups:

How soon did you start applying this advice?

Who's the person who told you this? Do you still have a relationship with him/her (may not be relevant, depending on context)

Why is this important to you?

How often do you remind yourself of it?

Do you ever give this same advice to anyone else?

Best Used: This is a good question to ask mid-initial conversation. You'll learn some basics about a person which will help build a relationship.

17 WHAT IS SOMETHING YOU'VE ALWAYS WANTED TO DO BUT HAVEN'T YET DONE?

Find out what's on his bucket list! Everyone has one, even when he doesn't have one.

Unless he's on his deathbed, everyone has some things he hasn't done that he wants to do.

This helps you learn someone's aspirations, goals, unfulfilled dreams, what he likes (or would like) to do for fun. Through this answer, you may be looking at the biggest void in his soul.

Follow Ups:

What's stopped you from doing it?

What do you imagine it would be like?

Who do you know who did it already?

How do you think you would feel after you've done it?

What would be next on your list after doing this?

Best Used: Use this in your initial conversation. This is a wide open question which allows a person to share a piece of exactly who he is.

18 IF YOU COULD HAVE LUNCH WITH ANYONE LIVING, WHO WOULD IT BE?

Who does she look up to? Ask yourself what that may mean. Then, ask her what it means.

Usually the "lunch" question leads to the naming of someone she admires. Often, it's the person she admires the most amongst people she doesn't actually know.

Follow Ups to dig deeper into the answer:

Where would you eat? Why?

What are the 3 burning questions you'd ask him/her?

Would you get a photo with him/her?

Would you want to stay in touch with this person? What would you offer in exchange for that continued contact?

Do you think this can happen in your lifetime? How would you make it happen if you had to make it happen?

Best Used: Use this when you want to take a conversation deeper, and when you have some time to keep talking. This isn't a hi-and-bye conversation question.

19 WHAT'S THE LAST ACTION OF YOURS THAT YOU REGRET?

Have someone tell you how he messed up, and you learn both what he values and what he doesn't approve of.

This is a really unique question that leads someone to recall recent actions, where the wound may still be fresh.

Where have you messed up recently?

Someone could also recall something small and insignificant when given the "recent" time constraint. If you're comfortable enough, challenge him for a bigger screw-up.

The answer you hear will help you learn what's of high importance to him. Is it family?

Work? The family dog? You also learn what types of things someone sees as a mistake - it could be the same action you would see as neutral, or even great!

Follow Ups:

Why the regret?

How would you do things differently?

Did the situation cost you anything?

Best Used: Once you've established rapport with someone, OR as an icebreaker with a brand new person.

20 WHAT ARE THE 3 BIGGEST MISCONCEPTIONS ABOUT (YOU OR WHAT YOU DO)?

I get to clear the air AND talk about myself, at the same time?! I thought you'd never ask!

This question is versatile, as every one of us knows our lives and work better than people on the outside looking in. And whenever we know we know something much better than others, we're just waiting for a chance to share that knowledge!

This question opens the door for that sharing. *Please correct the masses. They need it.*

No one can pass on this question, because we all have a *need* to answer it.

Follow Ups:

Why do you think people think that?

How do these misconceptions show themselves, besides just in conversation?

How often do you find yourself correcting people about _____?

Which one bothers you the most?

Best Used: When speaking to someone who is well-known in their environment - maybe locally, or famous to a specific niche group.

Or a person does something which we assume we understand (but probably don't - let him tell you). This applies to basically every vocation. Try it and see.

21 WHAT ARE THE MOST IMPORTANT THINGS ABOUT (YOU OR WHAT YOU DO) THAT MOST PEOPLE DON'T KNOW?

What is valuable about you that many people don't value? Where are your hidden gems?

Everyone has a story to share.

The main reason why you won't hear most peoples' stories, isn't because they don't know how to record a video or write a status update.

It's because no one ever asks, and so few people listen! Here's your opportunity to fill that void.

This question gets her to talk about what she sees as important, but doesn't get to express often. Listen closely and actively.

Follow Ups:

Why do you feel people don't know this about you or your work?

Why is it important to you?

If you wanted more people to know these things about you, how would you go about it?

Best Used: Great as a conversation opener, once formalities are out of the way.

This is a good way to get to know someone beyond the surface stuff we habitually share with people. Also note, this is something a person sees as important, but probably isn't ever asked about. They'll like you for offering the opportunity!

22 WHAT'S ONE THING YOU WISH YOU'D GET FROM THE PEOPLE IN YOUR LIFE, WHICH YOU DON'T CURRENTLY GET?

Get someone to tell you about the voids in his life.

We all have voids. Stuff we wish we had, but don't have. Our void could be people, energies, or material things.

The thing about voids, though, is we aren't (usually) freely open with sharing them. As adults, we've grown very skilled at showing what we want you to see, and hiding what we don't want seen. The trained eye, however, can easily spot what we try so hard to hide.

This conversation starter is for a person you feel is ready to share with you. Be careful not to use this one too soon.

Follow Ups:

Do you feel any of the people around you could *provide this if they were aware of your wants?*

How do you feel getting this would help you?

Have you ever given it yourself, to anyone else?

Best Used: Deep into a relationship or conversation with a person.

Don't use this until you have a feel you're talking to someone who has some trust in you (for whatever reason)!

I'm not telling you what's missing in *my* life unless I feel you have a sympathetic ear, or you can somehow provide or direct me to what I'm missing.

23 YOU'RE REALLY GOOD AT _____. HOW DID YOU DEVELOP THAT SKILL?

Ask what makes her so great. She will be happy to tell you.

Compliments to people are like the sun to flowers: We open up and angle our attention to the source of the warmth. Paying her a (genuine) compliment unlocks a person's need to share.

And yes - it *is* a NEED.

When you ask this question, the depth of the answer can vary depending on whom you ask.

Someone who is never asked this will open up so much as to appear like a young child telling you about their favorite toy.

A person who gets asked this often may have a rote answer, for which you can use one of the follow up questions below.

Follow Ups:

What has been most important for you to develop your ability?

If someone wanted to get started on your path today, where should he begin?

When/How did you realize you were better than most people at this?

Best Used: Could be used when you've just met a person, but really depends on how often she's been asked.

24 WHAT ARE YOU LISTENING TO THESE DAYS? MUSIC, PODCASTS, AUDIO?

What do you do for entertainment or in your leisure time?

Finding out what someone does when he's not working tells you a lot about him. Most all of us sleep and have some form of work. That extra, discretionary time, is what makes us unique.

Finding out what a man or woman does when he or she *could* do anything, tells us his interests, priorities, commitments, likes, and passions.

If you're aiming to build a relationship (and there's never a downside to doing so), those points are key knowledge.

Follow Ups:

How did you find out about that?

What's the #1 thing it does for you?

What would you recommend to me?

Best Used: This one is versatile enough to be used anytime, both with new acquaintances and familiar fiends.

25 WHERE WERE YOU IN _____ (CURRENT MONTH) _____ YEARS AGO?

Find out where he's been.

People have been through more stuff, and in more places, than they have time to tell you, or we have time to hear about. This question will open a door to those, when asked at the right time and in the right way.

Using this is a matter of feel, more than a systematic, do-it-at-this-time thing being prescribed to you.

You'll learn about someone's backstory, of course. You'll also get some information you probably didn't expect to learn about a person - if they're open to being asked by you!

Follow Ups:

Did you know back then that you'd be here, now?

What was the best part of that time period?

What would you have done differently back then?

Best Used: When you're talking to a person you've conversed with multiple times before and have talked beneath surface topics before.

ABOUT DRE BALDWIN

Dre Baldwin is the world's only expert on Mental Toughness, Confidence and Self-Discipline. A 9-year professional basketball player, Dre works with athletes, entrepreneurs and business professionals.

Dre has worked with Nike, Finish Line, Wendy's Gatorade, Buick, Wilson Sports and DIME magazine.

Dre has been blogging since 2005 and started publishing to YouTube in 2006. He has over 5,000 videos published, with daily content going out to his 115,000+ subscribers and being viewed over 35 million times. Dre's "Work On Your Game" show on Grant Cardone TV is consistently top-5 in views on the network.

Dre speaks, coaches and consults business professionals on mental toughness, confidence and discipline. He has given 3 TED Talks, published 7 books and has a daily podcast, Work On Your Game with DreAllDay. A Philadelphia native and Penn State alum, Dre lives in Miami.

Follow Dre -

Twitter & Periscope:

@DreAllDay

Instagram, SnapChat:

@DreBaldwin

READ MORE BY DRE BALDWIN,
INCLUDING:

Buy A Game
The Mental Handbook
Mirror Of Motivation
The Super You
The Overseas Basketball
Blueprint
Dre Philosophy Vol. 0
100 Mental Game Best Practices
25 Conversation Starters
55 Daily People Skills
25 Reasons To Quit Worrying

Made in the USA
Columbia, SC
16 July 2017